YOU CAN BEGIN AGAIN

DR. EMMANUEL K. BOTCHWAY

10-30-16

Don't close your case!

YOU CAN BEGIN AGAIN

DR. EMMANUEL K. BOTCHWAY

"Get up, don't give up."

"Once there is life, there is hope."

DR EMMANUEL K. BOTCHWAY

YOU CAN BEGIN AGAIN

DR. EMMANUEL K. BOTCHWAY

"OUR PROBLEM IS NOT FALLING DOWN, OUR REAL PROBLEM IS STAYING DOWN. LIFE HAPPENS, WE FALL DOWN, WE GET UP."

IT'S A MUST READ!

Dr. Emmanuel K. Botchway

You Can Begin Again

Emmanuel Botchway Ministries
1401 Pheasant Run Trail, Fort Worth, TX, 76131

All scriptures quotations are taken from the King James Version of the Holy Bible, unless otherwise stated.

Published by DiggyPod, United States of America
Printed in the United States of America
ISBN: 978-0-9969137-1-3

This book is printed on acid-free paper.
The views expressed in this work are solely those of the author and do not necessarily reflect the views of the publisher, and the publisher hereby disclaims any responsibility for them.

The author has made every effort to trace copyright holders, but if he has inadvertently overlooked any, he will be graceful to make changes in subsequent printing

Cover designed by Christian F. Sesay Jr.

CONTENT

DEDICATION

I dedicate this book to Abba Father, the Creator and the Maker of Heaven and Earth, the Most Wise God. In Him I live, move and have any being. To Him be all the glory in Jesus Name.

Also to my precious, and virtuous wife, mother (Mrs.) Annie Botchway, who is undeniably my greatest fan and supporter, thank you for believing in my vision. To my three brilliant, respectful and beautiful daughters: Irene, Emma and Elise. I love you much.

To my family and spiritual family, the holistic and dynamic members at Hope International Church and Ministries, for your prayer and unflinching support Hopers, you are too much! Thank you!

ACKNOWLEDGEMENTS

I wish to acknowledge and appreciate God through the power of the Holy Spirit for helping me to write this book. To my wife, Mrs. Annie Botchway, words aren't enough to thank you for serving as my personal secretary, and to Sis. Joselyne Guiguian, thank you for typing this book.

To the Emmanuel Botchway Ministries, sponsors and partners, thank you for your prayers, support, and financial contributions. Hope International Church and Ministries members, I couldn't have done this without you. I am grateful for all of your prayers and financial support.

To my editor, Dr. Christian F. Sesay Jr., thank you for editing and designing this book's cover.

To my publisher, and all those who in diverse ways the Lord has used to help me make this project a reality and a success. Thank you! As you have helped me, may you never lack destiny helpers in this life in Jesus' name. Amen!

INTRODUCTION

Dear beloved, it is an honor and a privilege for me to introduce this life-changing book to you as a spiritual and common sense guide that will help you navigate through some of the challenges life will throw at you.

Writing has always been a part of my life even before I was saved (born again). At a very early age, I began writing letters to family and friends all around the world. I wrote letters for my organizations and associations of all sorts while growing up. You may say but pastor "Everyone write letters." Yes, that is true. However, there was something more to my writings than meet the eyes. When you hear me speak, you will agree that I was born to communicate. But reading my writings will convince you beyond all reasonable doubt that I was gifted with the art of writing.

In 2013, the seed to write and publish was first sown in my heart by the Holy Spirit. In 2015, my first book, which entitled, "Who is Behind my Trouble" was written. After the success of that initial book, I knew that I was not just called to the four walls of the church, but to the four corners of the Earth through my writings as well.

As the senior pastor of Hope International Church and Ministries, I have been led by God to lead a local church with a monthly prophetic word, which gives the church a prophetic direction.

Surely the Lord GOD will do nothing, but He revealeth his secret unto his servants, the prophets. Amos 3:7

For the past six years, God has been guiding us with the prophetic word for our church family.

It is recorded in the Bible that the sons of Issachar were wise and led all of their brethren because they understood the times and the seasons as to what God was doing.

And of the children of Issachar, which were men that had understanding of the times, to know what Israel ought to do; the heads of them were two hundred; and all their brethren were at their commandment. 1 Chronicles 12:32

Also, in 1st Kings 17, the prophet Elijah, the Tishbite proclaimed a drought in Gilead. God spoke to him to go the brook of Cherith and he was going to take care of him there. After a season, the brook dried up and God spoke to him again to arise and go to Zarephath because he had prepared a widow there to take care of him. And in every season Elijah knew what to do because he was open to hearing the voice of God (a prophetic word)

No word, No direction

May I submit to you that you need a word from God to fulfill your destiny on Earth. Supposed Elijah did not hear the voice of God, he would have missed his next level in life. It is my prayers for you that you will not miss the prophetic voice of God for your next level. In Jesus' Name, Amen!

In August 2015, this book "You Can Begin Again" was birth. Eight is the prophetic number symbolizing new beginning. I was led by God to decree and declare in August 2015 as our month of new beginnings. It was at that point that the Lord began to speak to me to write this book. When He instructed me to write, I began to write. He told me how He has seen His people struggling when they fall down and He wanted them to know that they could begin again despite their predicament. He wanted to use me to let His people of whom you are a part of know that they can begin again. No matter what has happened to you in life, no matter how many times you have failed or fallen, you can always begin again. The Lord said to me, "Son, would you go and encourage, educate and empower my people that it doesn't matter, their past will not determine their future. Behold old things have passed away and all things are being new."

For to him that is joined to all the living there is hope: for a living dog is better than a dead lion. Ecclesiastes 9:4

Knowledge is power.

I know that this book will transform lives and renew minds. It will revolutionize your spirit to begin again. I say to you dear that it is not over until it is over. As you read through the pages of this book, may the spirit behind the letters help you to begin again.

In addition to this message that God has given me for this generation, I have always used the scriptures (the Word of God) and His wisdom and revelation to write. However, this time, the Lord has inspired me to use in this book real people and their stories and to make this book very practical to everyday living.

Let's pray. Dear Heavenly Father, in the name of Jesus, I pray as I read this book "You Can Begin Again", help me to begin again by your power and by Your spirit. In Jesus Name. Amen.

CHAPTER 1
SPIRITUALITY

In this chapter, I would like to deal with our spirituality and all the spirits of men and women. Beginning again, begins with our spirit and our spirituality. Man is a three part being (tripartite); spirit, soul, and body. Let's define our spirit in order to move on. Our spirit is defined as the invisible, nonmaterial (non-physical) part of a person. We are a spirit (God breathe), we have a soul (our mind, will and emotion) and we live in a frame (our body). The real you is your spirit and at death your body will go back to the dust. Your soul (mind) will cease to exist and your spirit wills live for eternity either in Heaven or Hell. Our spirit never dies.

And the very God of peace sanctify you wholly; and I pray God your whole spirit and soul and body be preserved blameless unto the coming of our Lord Jesus Christ. 1 Thessalonians 5:23

Then shall the dust return to the earth as it was: and the spirit shall return unto God who gave it. Ecclesiastes 12:7

The spirit of man is the candle of the Lord, searching all the inward parts of the belly. Proverbs 20:27

Everything begins and ends with your spirit. You are your spirit. To begin again, your spirit man must be intact. Spiritually speaking, your spirit man is the source of your strength in God. Therefore, to begin again spiritually, few things have to happen. Please note that in the book of the beginnings, Genesis, God said this…

And the Lord God commanded the man, saying, Of every tree of the garden thou mayest freely eat: 17 But of the tree of the knowledge of good and evil, thou shalt not eat of it: for in the day that thou greatest thereof thou shalt surely die. Genesis 2:16-17

Now please understand that when God said to Adam and Eve, that the day you eat of the fruit of this tree you shall surely die, He meant spiritually. How do I know that? Because God is not a man that He should lie, if He says a thing, He will do it. Now after Adam and Eve disobeyed God and ate the fruit, they died spiritually and not physically because as you and I know they continued to live on physically. But they died spiritually (separation from God). That is why every man or woman born through Adam and Eve are born into sin and is spiritually dead. In order for mankind to be reconciled and restored to God, we have to be born again (spiritual rebirth).

Jesus answered and said unto him, Verily, verily, I say unto thee, Except a man be born again, he cannot see the kingdom of God. John 3:3
Therefore the first thing to beginning again in God is to be born again. May I submit to you that, if you are not born again, saved or a Christian you need to be born again in order to begin again spiritually.
Purge out therefore the old leaven, that ye may be a new lump, as ye are unleavened. For even Christ our passover is sacrificed for us: 1 Corinthians 5:7

Secondly, and as a Christian, we make mistakes from time to time, backslide, miss the mark, sin and fall but it is written in the Holy Book:
If we say that we have no sin, we deceive ourselves, and the truth is not in us. If we confess our sins, he is faithful and just to forgive us our sins, and to cleanse us from all unrighteousness. If we say that we have not sinned, we make him a liar, and his word is not in us. 1 John 1:8-10

Therefore as Christians (children of God), when we sin we must confess our sins to God in order for us to begin again. Also in the book of Psalms, King David prayed this prayer of repentance so that he could begin again…

Have mercy upon me, O God, according to thy loving kindness: according unto the multitude of thy tender mercies blot out my transgressions. Wash me thoroughly from mine iniquity, and cleanse me from my sin. For I acknowledge my transgressions: and my sin is ever before me. Against thee, thee only, have I sinned, and done this evil in thy sight: that thou mightest be justified when thou speakest, and be clear when thou judgest. Behold, I was shapen in iniquity; and in sin did my mother conceive me. Behold, thou desirest truth in the inward parts: and in the hidden part thou shalt make me to know wisdom. Purge me with hyssop, and I shall be clean: wash me, and I shall be whiter than snow. Make me to hear joy and gladness; that the bones, which thou hast broken, may rejoice. Hide thy face from my sins, and blot out all mine iniquities. Create in me a clean heart, O God; and renew a right spirit within me. Cast me not away from thy presence; and take not thy holy spirit from me. Restore unto me the joy of thy salvation; and uphold me with thy free spirit. Then will I teach transgressors thy ways; and sinners shall be converted unto thee. Deliver me from blood guiltiness, O God, thou God of my salvation: and my tongue shall sing aloud of thy righteousness. O Lord, open thou my lips; and my mouth shall shew forth thy praise. For thou desirest not sacrifice; else would I give it: thou delightest not in burnt offering. The sacrifices of God are a broken spirit: a broken and a contrite heart, O God, thou wilt not despise. Do good in thy good pleasure unto Zion: build thou the walls of Jerusalem. Then shalt thou be pleased with the sacrifices of righteousness, with burnt offering and whole burnt offering: then shall they offer bullocks upon thine altar. Psalms 51: 1-19

Beloved, our God is merciful and slow to anger. There is nothing we have done or can do that when we repent, He will not forgive us. He is rich in mercy and full of grace. He will forgive you and give you another chance. I am not just writing this chapter from the position of a head knowledge or mere educational standpoint, I am a living example and a testimony of how good, loving, and merciful our God is. I am a beneficiary of not only His saving mercy but also His forgiving grace. He has given me another, and another, and another chance to begin again and that is why I am writing this book encouraging you to believe that you too can begin again.

As a good Bible student, you will notice that King David wrote Psalms 51 after he had committed adultery with Uriah's wife, Bathsheba, and murdered Uriah and took his wife in 2nd Samuel 11. But when King David acknowledged his sins and repented asking God for forgiveness, God forgave David and he began again. I encourage you by the mercies of God, that nothing you have done is too bad for God to forgive you. You can begin again. If King David after all he had done is still called "the Man after God's Own Heart", there is hope for us my brothers and sisters.

Thirdly, in this journey of life, things happen. When we fall down, we get up. The Christian journey is a glorious and wonderful one, yet at the same time it has its own ups and downs, twists and turns. But the journey continues! The wise man Solomon once wrote…

For a just man falleth seven times, and riseth up again: but the wicked shall fall into mischief.
Proverbs 24:16

My dear readers let me be clear with you, God is not happy when we fall, but He has a problem when we stay down. Our real problem in life is not falling down, because everyone reading this book I believe have either fallen before or fail in some manner or way. The real problem is staying down.

We fall down. We get up.

Precious ones, you can begin again, let me share with you few men and women in the Bible who fell down and got up again. Moses committed murder in Egypt but God called him the deliverer. David committed adultery and murder but God called him the Man after His own heart. Rehab was a prostitute but God used her in the lineage of Jesus Christ our Lord and Savior. The women caught in adultery, Jesus called her His daughter and we later learned that she served and followed Him. Paul persecuted the Christians but Jesus used him to write more than half of the New Testament and entrusted the great message of grace into his hands for us the gentiles. There is hope for you. You can begin again spiritually!

My dear readers please don't get me wrong I am not justifying or encouraging sin, I am writing about the grace and the mercy of God to begin again. Right teaching will lead to right believing, and right believing will lead to right living.

Let's pray. If you are not born again (Christian) please say this prayer aloud. Dear Lord Jesus, I know I'm a sinner and I ask you to forgive me from all my sins. I believe you died for my sins and rose from the dead. Help me to trust and follow you as my Lord and Savior. Guide my life and help me to live for you. Amen.

Beloved, if you pray this prayer you are now born again. Welcome to the family of God. Find a Bible believing church and become a part of God's kingdom, serve Him, give to kingdom work, believe in His word, and live for Him.

If you are already a Christian and you have backslidden and you want to rededicate your life to the Lord, please say this prayer out loud:
Dear Lord Jesus, I know I have not been living for you to the best of my abilities. I have backslidden. Today I repent and rededicate my life to you. Please create in me a clean heart and renew a right spirit within, restore to me the joy of my salvation. In Jesus name!

Now my brothers and sisters go and make first things first and do the right thing. I encourage you to begin to go to church, find a ministry to serve in, read your Bible, pray and fast, give your tithes and give to the work of God. Draw closer to God and He will draw closer to you.

To those of us who are saved and have not backslide, but are struggling in our relationship and work with God. *Please pray this prayer out loud. Dear Lord Jesus, increase my faith. I pray for wisdom and strength to keep on living for you. Please help me and encourage my heart along this journey. In Jesus' name.*

CHAPTER 2

THE DEATH OF A LOVED ONE

In this chapter I will be dealing with the death of a loved one, namely husband, wife, children, mother, father, siblings, relatives or close friends. I want to believe that this chapter will be one of the most challenging chapters for me to write, simply because of the mystery and seriousness of death. Death is truly a mystery that men has not come to understand and will never make sense of it until…

Death is simply defined as ceasing to exist physically and or the end of our physical life. A loved one can be defined as a person we are related to or people we care about deeply with emotions and affections. Death can be devastating; it ends once life and ruins and disrupts other lives in the process. That is why this chapter was written. To remind you about the challenges that comes alongside the death of a loved one. I don't think we can solve all of deaths problems, but I believe that we can be empowered and equipped to make peace with death and we can begin again after losing a loved one. Many lives have been destroyed by the loss of a loved one. Destinies have been aborted because of the death of a closed family member or friend but you can begin again.

Yes I want to admit that death can be devastating, and the effect of death can paralyze one. However, by the Grace of God and His peace that surpasses all understanding we can obtain wisdom and find strength to begin again. We can get spiritual counseling, the church, family and friends support and other resources like this to help us move on with life.

> We keep on living for both the dead and the living.

I am writing this chapter to minister to three groups of people. The first group, are people who have lost a loved one and have walked that dark and lonely road of life but have found the strength and the grace to keep on living regardless of their loss. I encourage you to keep on living for "them"- your lost loved ones.

The second group is those people who have lost loved one(s) and is going through difficult times right now. They don't even know how to make it from day to day, I write to encourage you. I acknowledge that no two situations or circumstances are the same and to say I understand what you are going through will be an understatement, but I submit to you that you will survive and begin again.

For to him that is joined to all the living there is hope: for a living dog is better than a dead lion. Ecclesiastes 9:4

But now thus saith the Lord that created thee, O Jacob, and he that formed thee, O Israel, Fear not: for I have redeemed thee, I have called thee by thy name; thou art mine. When thou passest through the waters, I will be with thee; and through the rivers, they shall not overflow thee: when thou walkest through the fire, thou shalt not be burned; neither shall the flame kindle upon thee. For I am the Lord thy God, the Holy One of Israel, thy Saviour: I gave Egypt for thy ransom, Ethiopia and Seba for thee. Isaiah 43:1-3

Be strong and of a good courage, fear not, nor be afraid of them: for the Lord thy God, he it is that doth go with thee; he will not fail thee, nor forsake thee. Deuteronomy 31:6

It is my prayers for you that you will not only survive but that you will thrive and go on to doing great exploits in this life. You can begin again! I encourage you to look up to the hills, from whence comes your help, your help comes from God who made the Heavens and the Earth.

The third group, are people who don't have any clue of what group one and two have been through or is going through. This group is in their waiting season. Therefore, I pray that in your times of trouble, this book would have empowered and equipped you to press through life's journey. I hate to admit this, but

I have to because it is the truth. One day, someway, somehow a loved one will die, be strong and encourage life does not end at the death of a loved one. You will survive and you can begin again.

As I begin to pray and plan to write this book, I asked God for wisdom and direction. He impressed upon my heart to not only use scriptures, revelations and biblical saints, but to use real people in time who have or is living this reality.

> We are real people, living in a real world, with real issues, serving a real God and is attacked by a real devil.

So God told me, "Son, I want you to look around and you will find people in your family, church and your community who have and is living these chapters and use them as a living example to encourage and challenge your readers that it is possible to begin again after the loss of a loved one."

And David said unto Nathan, I have sinned against the Lord. And Nathan said unto David, The Lord also hath put away thy sin; thou shalt not die. Howbeit, because by this deed thou hast given great occasion to the enemies of the Lord to blaspheme, the child also that is born unto thee shall surely die. And Nathan departed unto his house. And the Lord struck the child that Uriah's wife bare unto David, and it was very sick. David therefore besought God for the child; and David fasted, and went in, and lay all night upon the earth. And the elders of his house arose, and went to him, to raise him up from the earth: but he would not, neither did he eat bread with them. And it came to pass on the seventh day that the child died. And the servants of David feared to tell him that the child was dead: for they said, Behold, while the child was yet alive, we spake unto him, and he would not hearken unto our voice: how will he then vex himself, if we tell him that the child is dead? But when David saw that his servants whispered, David perceived that the child was dead: therefore David said unto his servants, is the child dead? And they said, He is dead. Then David arose from the earth, and washed, and anointed himself, and changed his apparel, and came into the house of the Lord, and worshipped: then he came to his own house; and when he required, they set bread before him, and he did eat. Then said his servants unto him, what thing is this that thou hast done? Thou didst fast and weep for the child, while it was alive; but when the child was dead, thou didst rise and eat bread. And he said, while the child was yet alive, I fasted and wept: for I said, who can tell whether God will be gracious to me, that the child may live? But now he is dead, wherefore should I fast? Can I bring him back again? I shall go to him, but he shall not return to me. 2 Samuel 12: 13-23

This is a classical true-life biblical account about King David, Bathsheba and their sick son. This story is a practical lesson about losing a child and moving on. Losing a loved one at any level or account is painful, not to talk about losing a child.

It has been said no parent should bury their child. But yet parents are burying their children today, it is a sad truth, however life goes on.

I will like to introduce a mother who lost her child, her first born in his mid-twenties. This is a true and real life story. Mrs. Doris Bangura Bright, a wife, a mother and a leader. Sister Doris is one of the founding members and leader at Hope International Church and Ministries in Hurst, Texas. Where I am her spiritual father and pastor.

It was in October of 2010, when I received that call, I can still remember, like it just happened. It was in the morning hours and I was at work. I received this call from a woman named Doris frantically saying, "my son Unisa is dead." My initial responses were "Wow!" "What!" "When?" "What happened?" I was also in shock and had to leave work immediately. I rushed to her house only to confirm my worse nightmare. It was true, the young man had passed away.

It was a sad day for many. For Doris, no words could describe the state of mind she was in and all of the what if's question that were going through her mind. it was the beginning of a long process but with God's help and the help from family and friends and her church community at large, she took it one day at a time. Putting first things first, funeral arrangements were made, planning the wake, funeral and burial.

After everything had subsided, the visits reduced, the calls got fewer and fewer, reality set in. But Life had to go on and that she needed to begin again for herself and her only surviving son. So she learned to live for both the son that is gone and the surviving son. It was a one-day at a time journey. On some days, she was up and in other days, she was down. No one can fully explain the frame of mind of a grieving mother considering society's expectation of children burying their parents.

She did not, will not and can never forget her son. And that is understandable. After all, what parent will erase the memory of their lost child easily? To this day, she still feels the pain from time to time and the vacuum the absence of this promising young man has created. Even though she carries his memories in a special place in her heart, yet she has learned through it all to begin again because life goes on.

I write to encourage someone today who has lost a child or children, it is sad, the hurts and the pains are real, the memories keep living on but you can learn to begin again. May the story of Doris encourage, strengthen, bless and challenge you to accept and make peace with the reality of life. I pray that God will help you to begin again in Jesus' name.

And the Lord God said, it is not good that the man should be alone; I will make him a help meet for him. And out of the ground the Lord God formed every beast of the field, and every fowl of the air; and brought them unto Adam to see what he would call them: and whatsoever Adam called every living creature that was the name thereof. And Adam gave names to all cattle, and to the fowl of the air, and to every beast of the field; but for Adam there was not found a help meet for him. And the Lord God caused a deep sleep to fall upon Adam, and he slept: and he took one of his ribs, and closed up the flesh instead thereof; And the rib, which the Lord God had taken from man, made he a woman, and brought her unto the man. And Adam said, this is now bone of my bones, and flesh of my flesh: she shall be called Woman, because she was taken out of Man. Therefore shall a man leave his father and his mother, and shall cleave unto his wife: and they shall be one flesh. And they were both naked, the man and his wife, and were not ashamed. Genesis 2: 18-35

I would like to introduce to you another young lady who was stricken by the devastations of the loss of a loved one. Her name is Blawin. She was 26 years old and my spiritual daughter. She is a committed chorister at my church and a faithful and loyal young lady. She was very sweet and respectful. Blawin dated this young and handsome and very promising young man, Konah, who I also took as a son. They both dated for about 6 years and their relationship was blessed with a beautiful girl, Bridgette. When they approached me that they were ready to tie the nuptial knot, they said, "Pastor, we have dated for a while and have been blessed with this beautiful daughter, life has been good to us and everything is working together for our good. We will like to take this relationship to the next level by getting married." I was happy as always when young couples express their desire to get married. We arranged premarital counseling and begun planning for the wedding. They completed their counseling and the day came and they got married. Life for them has just begun, the future was bright, they had many dreams and plans, things to do, places to go, people to see and they were just so in love.

It was about 3 months into their marriage when one morning her husband, Konah woke up, had a talk with her and left for work that Tuesday with the understanding that he was coming back home the next day. Konah was a CDL certified truck driver. The next day the sheriff came to their house and told Blawin that her husband, Konah was involved in a fatal motor accident and that they were sorry to inform her that he did not make it..

Blawin's world came crumbling down. For a young lady with a three-year old daughter who had married for only 3 months to become a widow was simply as terrible as it can get. Her whole life was about to take a different turn. In her phone call to me, she yelled, "Pastor, Konah. Konah. Konah was in an accident and the police are here telling me that he died." In shock and disbelief, I hurried to their home and asked the sheriff what was the real story. He told me exactly what they had told Blawin that Konah was involved in a fatal truck accident and did not make it.

It was a very difficult season for everyone, not to mention Blawin and her daughter, Bridgette. Konah's parents and siblings were equally devastated. I have never been so distraught about a death like this ever. It was a tragedy in our community. Blawin and the family had to learn to begin again one day at a time. The road was long, dark, lonely, painful, hurtful, depressing and the list goes on. Once again Blawin had to keep living for herself, their daughter and for Konah.

As I write to you now, I am excited to you inform you that in a recent memorial service held for Konnah last September, even though you could still tell from the memorial service that the pain and hurt over the death of Konnah continue to linger on, but on the whole Blawin and her little daughter, as well as the rest of the family, the church, and the community have since found the peace, joy, strength and the faith to move on and keep on keeping on. Blawin was able to sing a solo in as a tribute to her deceased husband. Her voice was anointed and powerful and many wondered and broke out into giving God praise and thanks for how far the Lord has brought her. You can tell that she was beginning to begin again. She expressed thanksgiving to God and gratitude to all who in one way or the other have been there for her through the past year. She emphasized that it was God's grace and strength that saw her through. Please don't misunderstand me, it was not an easy journey.

The road to beginning again was long, dark and lonely, but by the grace of God and family and friends, she came to a place when she could make peace for her lost and find hope and strength to move on. I submit to you, you too can begin again. May you find a reason to live, love and laugh again. May the story of this young lady encourage, bless and give you the hope to live and begin again. Amen.

The next piece of real story is about a wonderful and prayerful woman of God. A woman whose obsession and unparalleled faithfulness to the Lord is second to none. She is Deaconess Margaret. When she lost her late husband Tom who was commonly or affectionately called Uncle Tom by many of us. Uncle Tom was a man that was full of life and energy. Deaconess Margaret's story t oh how she moved on after such a devastating loss will encourage many that regardless of our present circumstances, it is possible to begin again.

> Bad things can happen to good people.

While he was yet speaking, there came also another, and said, Thy sons and thy daughters were eating and drinking wine in their eldest brother's house: And, behold, there came a great wind from the wilderness, and smote the four corners of the house, and it fell upon the young men, and they are dead; and I only am escaped alone to tell thee. Then Job arose, and rent his mantle, and shaved his head, and fell down upon the ground, and worshipped. Job 1:18-20

She and her husband were married for almost 29 years. And, the union was blessed with two children; Delarose and Tom Jr. Delarose is deceased now and Tom Jr is alive, doing well and bubbling. Uncle Tom had relocated to the United States to join his wife. He was an army veteran and very outgoing and a disciplinarian. He was preparing to go into the seminary to study prior to his illness.

He had some struggles with ulcer at certain time in his life when he in 2009, he was diagnosed with cancer of the stomach. After this scary diagnosis and life altering moment, he underwent a surgery that was deemed very successful. But little pockets of the cancer continued to plague him in later years. He struggled with this illness for about 3 years when in 2012, he finally succumbed to death. The community had lost one of its heroes.

For a wife losing her husband of 29 years together in marital bliss stinks and was painful. The pain, the hurt, the struggles, the memories were just too much to bear. At some point she decided this would be my story. She began to settle with her realities. But somewhere along her difficult to understand journey, she learned that through it all she can begin again. I taught and encouraged her to believe that she can begin again: that she can learn to live, to love, and to laugh again.

She dared to believe that it was possible to begin again. I would like to share with you that through all of her pains and hurt, she memorialized her late husband. Today, with great joy in my heart, I would like to share with you that Deaconess Margaret has begun again; she is happily married again and now lives with her husband in Atlanta, Georgia. Yes she was hurt, the pains were real, the memories will continue but she has come to the understanding that life has to go on. She can live, love and laugh again. May her story inspire, encourage and challenge you to begin again.

Let us pray. Please say this pray aloud with me. Lord Jesus, I come to you confessing that he death of my loved one(s)… (say their name) … has hurt me. I come to you today for help to move on. Your word says that Your Grace is sufficient for me in every situation, oh Lord, let Your grace rest upon me and I pray for Your peace that surpass all understanding will guide my heart. Lord Jesus I surrender my heart and hurt to You, please heal my heart, renew my mind and help me to find peace and strength to move on. I want to live, love, and laugh again. Thank you Lord Jesus, I receive strength and hope to begin again. In Jesus' Name.

CHAPTER 3

DIVORCE OR BREAKUPS

Like every other chapter in this book, many people are devastated and discouraged in life for obviously many reasons. In this chapter, I intend to examine one of the most difficult moments in one's life- divorces and break ups. Because of the debilitating effects of divorces and all of its attendant havocs dumped on a person's life, it is placed second to death in the rankings of atrocities in human life. Divorces, inarguably has a greater propensity to destroy, damage, devastate, and disrupt one's life. Divorce is painful and hurtful. It paralyzes the future of not just the couples involved, but the children caught up in the middle and the family and friends connected to them.

Many people's lives have changed because of the unfriendly impact of divorce. Usually, after hotly contentious divorces, the reactions manifest some people stopped pursuing life. For some, depression and bitterness sinks in, while some refuse to trust anyone again. They have vowed never to love or trust a partner ever again. I do understand that not every divorce is as devastating and damaging as one might be tempted to think. In some relationships, couples have found amicable ways of dissolving their marriages. However, for the vast majority, it is not so simple.

Due to this very touchy reality of life, God has anointed and entrusted me with the knowledge and revelation to encourage and empower you to begin again. I therefore write that while it is true that all of the effects of divorces are true and real, yet a greater truth and reality is that you can begin again.

Many have vowed not to ever get married again. Some have even said, “I will never trust a partner again.” Few have said, “I will never truly love anyone again, the way I loved him or her.” This book has come for all to say that even though it hurts because it happened, I can always begin again.

Because of the sensitivity of this subject, I have chosen not to use the real names of a particular couple who went through significant challenges in dealing with life after divorce. This couple married for more than a decade with four beautiful children.

The marriage was no longer working, as they had wanted. Every effort, counseling, and intervention to rescue their marriage failed. After exhausting every possible avenues to arrest their declining marriage, the couple gave up. When they decided to pursue a divorce, the nightmare started. Their home became the theatre for fighting, name calling, and the rest…. The couple's life and those of their once promising children took a turn for the worst. They embarked on a long, dark and painful road. Wasting money on legal fees, compromising their children's mental sanity, and family and friends were not spared from the mess. It was a bitter experience for the couples and those associated with them. At the time of the couple's nightmare, none of them wanted to ever get involve again in another relationship.

After few years, I am pleased to inform you that each of the couple has remarried to someone else. They are both living happily in separate lives. One of them even had another child. Talking to them, they are quick to tell you about how God always have a way of making sense out of nonsense, turning pain into praise and turning your mess into a message. The couple's hurt was turned into strength and it is that strength that they leaned on to begin again. You too can begin again!

They said to me separately, "Please write our story so that many can be encouraged to begin again. We have a reason to keep on keeping on." One of them said, "I never knew that I could be this happy again." The other said, "After going through child support, I doubted if I were going to have another child again, but here I am planning to have another one. Life is good! It is not over until it is over." I dare you to believe that regardless of what had happened, you can live, love, trust, laugh, and play again.

Beloved, I don't have all the answers to life and I am not trying to give answers here. All that the Lord has asked me to do is to write and encourage you that as long as there is life, there is hope. Keep on keeping on! Maybe you even did all the right things, but yet the marriage ended up the way it did, please be encouraged. When one door closes, another door opens. I know it's easier said than done, but please read this scripture and let it encourage your heart.

For this thing I besought the Lord thrice that it might depart from me. And he said unto me, My grace is sufficient for thee: for my strength is made perfect in weakness. Most gladly therefore will I rather glory in my infirmities, that the power of Christ may rest upon me. 2 Corinthians 12:8-9

BREAK-UPS

Break-ups, break-ups, break-ups! It is a drama like none other. Even though some might say that it is a milder version of divorce, yet it can be problematic in its own ways. While it is true, it cannot be compared to divorce, it has its own dynamics and serious effects.

Break-ups are very damaging for these simple but tangible reasons – if not careful it can shape and tint the heart, creating memories on the minds of young

First impression goes a long way.

lovers for a long time. Break-ups can have a lasting effect for so many reasons.

More than half of the break-ups that take place happen between young and or inexperienced couples. Many are in love, and are innocent and naïve. Some are in lust, infatuation, fantasy and the likes. They are inclined to believe that just because they are in love, everything will work itself out and so they give their hearts out. I guess hoping and praying that nothing will go wrong. But when things do not go the way they had hoped for and there is a sudden break-up for whatever reason, their whole worldview on life, love and relationship can be challenged. It is said that the first experience trying something new can determine whether you'd continue to do it.

I guess my assignment in this chapter is not to explain the why and the why nots, who's right and who's wrong in those break ups. My responsibility is to educate and submit to you that break ups do happen and it can be very troubling and disturbing. However, through it all I encourage you that you can begin again.

> Break-ups can either teach you for future relationships or cheat you of future relationship.

If you seek my personal opinion as it relates to divorces and break ups, I will answer this question: Why do I think that break ups can be more problematic compared to divorces? Because break ups can shape and mold our minds for the future you want or desire. I think most of our first, or early childhood experiences shaped our future.

I have heard many good love stories. Stories of love at first sight that took many breathe away. High school sweethearts who were meant for each other and marriages made in heaven. These stories were true and they have happened and still happening.

Fall in love with your heart and your mind.

However, the reality of life and the real truth is many of us had to go through break ups as we progressed in life. Some were easy, others were hurtful and some were very devastating. No matter what your own fair share of experience is, you can begin again.

Let me close this chapter with a simple advice from the depth of my knowledge and experience. Life is not a straight line; it has its own twists and turns, ups and downs, make-ups and break ups.

Your first love should not be your last love.

All of our expectations in life do not always come to manifestation. Things do happen in life and every plan does not go as expected. Some disappointments might be blessings in disguise. Be real!

R – Realistic

E – Expectation

A – About

L – Life

> Love will always be love.

I want you to love hard and be opened again. And, to have faith and believe in your relationships. In a similar vein, I also want you to be prepared for the unexpected. I wish I could tell you that because your love is true and sincere, nothing can go wrong. But I would be lying if I do. A young sister introduced me to a video titled "After Us". In the video, a young couple broke up after a three-year relationship. While the story only gives the perspective of the young lady; it shows the steps and experiences that come with a break up such as the memories. There are days that you just don't want to face the world or care about your looks, the tears and the anticipation on a call or text. You have to understand that's just how life goes and you have

> Fall in love with your heart and your senses.

to go through the first stage of reminiscing and retracting (some take longer than others in this stage). Stage two is releasing, where you pick up yourself, dress cute and suppress urges to go back to stage one, and lastly step three, which is rebuilding. In this stage, you meet new people, socialize, flirt and do things towards the better of you.

I want to encourage you that no matter what had happened in your relationships, you can survive and you can begin again. Wishing you the best of luck and blessings in your new or next relationship.

Let's pray. Please say this prayer out loud with me. Lord Jesus, I come to you today confessing that I am hurt and bitter from my divorce and or breakup,

I confess it has affected or is affecting me. Please help me to move on, heal my heart, my hurt, restore my confidence and give me the courage to love and trust again. I want to love again, trust again, laugh again, and spend the rest of my life with someone who will love me in return and respect and cherish me. So help me God. Thank you Lord for the courage and the strength to begin again. Amen.

CHAPTER 4

TERMINAL ILLNESS

Now a certain man was sick, named Lazarus, of Bethany, the town of Mary and her sister Martha. (It was that Mary which anointed the Lord with ointment, and wiped his feet with her hair, whose brother Lazarus was sick.) Therefore his sisters sent unto him, saying, Lord, behold, he whom thou lovest is sick. When Jesus heard that, he said, this sickness is not unto death, but for the glory of God, that the Son of God might be glorified thereby.
John 11: 1-4

This chapter is dedicated to those whose lives have been altered or interrupted by illnesses due to natural causes or accidents. These can be very difficult times in anyone's life. Once upon a time, you were the epitome of health, up and running, bubbling and kicking, living life to the fullest and pursing your dreams. But one day, you got up and life was never the same. For some, the feelings of sickness were attributed to the normal aches and body pains until a visit was made to the doctor. When results came back after the usual running of diagnostic tests, life will never be the same again. It seemed as the beginning of hell on earth.

Many during these difficult times will throw in the towel and some will go as far as writing life off.

> In life we can either run to the finish line, walk to the finish line, hop to the finish line or crawl to the finish line, either way, make it anyhow.

Some will stop living and start dying. Today, please be encouraged that sometimes in life we all get dealt with a bad and wrong card. You can call the game off or throw down your card and walk away or you can keep playing the hand you were dealt with to the best of your ability, In life, anything can happen but it should go on. May this book inspire and embolden you to remember that is not over until it is over.

A true story of a pastor demonstrated the power of God's strong hands? Pastor Nick, was alive and well, devoting his time and energy, pursing the call of God on his life. All of a sudden, just like the Bible recorded in the book of Job, Pastor Nick fell ill and life for him and his family took a nose-dive deep turn for the worse. During such challenging moments in Pastor Nick's life, he could have asked several questions regarding the mercies of God. But no one doubted His power. Instead, Pastor Nick and family prayed and played the card that was dealt to them. His family kept on living to the best of their abilities.

Like Pastor Nick's predicament, Illness can change the course of one's life and if not handled properly it can worsen your condition. This is not to make light of this life altering circumstances, but it is to give you encouragement and hope to power through life regardless.

There are two groups that I would like to deal with in this chapter. The first group is those who became ill but were able to be healed.

In those days was Hezekiah sick unto death. And the prophet Isaiah the son of Amoz came to him, and said unto him, Thus saith the Lord, Set thine house in order; for thou shalt die, and not live. Then he turned his face to the wall, and prayed unto the Lord, saying, I beseech thee, O Lord, remember now how I have walked before thee in truth and with a perfect heart, and have done that which is good in thy sight. And Hezekiah wept sore. And it came to pass, afore Isaiah was gone out into the middle court, that the word of the Lord came to him, saying, Turn again, and tell Hezekiah the captain of my people, Thus saith the Lord, the God of David thy father, I have heard thy prayer, I have seen thy tears: behold, I will heal thee: on the third day thou shalt go up unto the house of the Lord. And I will add unto thy days fifteen years; and I will deliver thee and this city out of the hand of the king of Assyria; and I will defend this city for mine own sake, and for my servant David's sake. 2 Kings 20: 1-6

In the scripture above, we come to find out that Hezekiah became ill but God was able to heal him. I want to encourage you, yes you might be ill today and your life may have taken a different turn but God is able to heal you.

And when Jesus was passed over again by ship unto the other side, much people gathered unto him: and he was nigh unto the sea. And, behold, there cometh one of the rulers of the synagogue, Jairus by name; and when he saw him, he fell at his feet, And besought him greatly, saying, My little daughter lieth at the point of death: I pray thee, come and lay thy hands on her, that she may be healed; and she shall live. And Jesus went with him; and much people followed him, and thronged him. And a certain woman, which had an issue of blood twelve years, And had suffered many things of many physicians, and had spent all that she had, and was nothing bettered, but rather grew worse, When she had heard of Jesus, came in the press behind, and touched his garment. For she said, if I may touch but his clothes, I shall be whole. And straightway the fountain of her blood was dried up;

and she felt in her body that she was healed of that plague. And Jesus, immediately knowing in himself that virtue had gone out of him, turned him about in the press, and said, who touched my clothes? And his disciples said unto him, Thou seest the multitude thronging thee, and sayest thou, who touched me? And he looked round about to see her that had done this thing. But the woman fearing and trembling, knowing what was done in her, came and fell down before him, and told him all the truth. And he said unto her, Daughter, thy faith hath made thee whole; go in peace, and be whole of thy plague. Mark 5: 21-34

My purpose of quoting these scriptures is intentional. I want you to read the scriptures because only the word of God can bring the change you need in your life, bless and heal your life. In the passage above, this woman was ill and the challenges associated with her circumstances altered her life in so many ways. The scripture brings out the point that she spent all her living on this illness and still could not get well. But she did not give up. She kept pressing because she believes life goes on and Jesus will eventually heal her and He did.

After this there was a feast of the Jews; and Jesus went up to Jerusalem. Now there is at Jerusalem by the sheep market a pool, which is called in the Hebrew tongue Bethesda, having five porches. In these lay a great multitude of impotent folk, of blind, halt, withered, waiting for the moving of the water. For an angel went down at a certain season into the pool, and troubled the water: whosoever then first after the troubling of the water stepped in was made whole of whatsoever disease he had. And a certain man was there, which had an infirmity thirty and eight years. When Jesus saw him lie, and knew that he had been now a long time in that case, he saith unto him, Wilt thou be made whole? The impotent man answered him, Sir, I have no man, when the water is troubled, to put me into the pool: but while I am coming, another steppeth down before me. Jesus saith unto him, Rise, take up thy bed, and walk. And immediately the man was made whole, and took up his bed, and walked: and on the same day was the Sabbath. John 5:1-9

In this text, we see a man who was ill for almost 38 years. He did not give up, did not give in, and he stayed at the pool every day believing that today would be his day. This is the attitude that I am instilling in you; that you don't give up, you don't give in, and you believe that you can Begin Again. One day, this man received his healing; it is my prayer for you that one day you will receive your healing if you believe.

As I conclude this chapter, let me deal with the final group who got ill and lived with their illnesses. Life is real and we have to face it regardless of how gruesome it can become. Some get healed but some live through their illnesses.

And he rose up that night, and took his two wives, and his two women servants, and his eleven sons, and passed over the ford Jabbok. And he took them, and sent them over the brook, and sent over that he had. And Jacob was left alone; and there wrestled a man with him until the breaking of the day. And when he saw that he prevailed not against him, he touched the hollow of his thigh; and the hollow of Jacob's thigh was out of joint, as he wrestled with him. And he said, let me go, for the day breaketh. And he said, I will not let thee go, except thou bless me. And he said unto him, What is thy name? And he said, Jacob. And he said, Thy name shall be called no more Jacob, but Israel: for as a prince hast thou power with God and with men, and hast prevailed. And Jacob asked him, and said, tell me, I pray thee, thy name. And he said, wherefore is it that thou dost ask after my name? And he blessed him there. And Jacob called the name of the place Peniel: for I have seen God face to face, and my life is preserved. And as he passed over Penuel the sun rose upon him, and he halted upon his thigh. Genesis 32: 22-31

In this story, Jacob had an encounter with an angel and after the fight, his hip got fractured and scripture recalls that he lived on like that. I guess the point I'm trying to make here is that sometimes in life we will learn to keep on moving even though we are hurting. When we don't feel as sparkling as we normally do, we continue to forge ahead.

And David said, Is there yet any that is left of the house of Saul, that I may shew him kindness for Jonathan's sake? And there was of the house of Saul a servant whose name was Ziba. And when they had called him unto David, the king said unto him, Art thou Ziba? And he said, Thy servant is he. And the king said, Is there not yet any of the house of Saul, that I may shew the kindness of God unto him? And Ziba said unto the king, Jonathan hath yet a son, which is lame on his feet. And the king said unto him, Where is he? And Ziba said unto the king, Behold, he is in the house of Machir, the son of Ammiel, in Lodebar. Then King David sent, and fetched him out of the house of Machir, the son of

Ammiel, from Lodebar. Now when Mephibosheth, the son of Jonathan, the son of Saul, was come unto David, he fell on his face, and did reverence. And David said, Mephibosheth. And he answered, Behold thy servant! And David said unto him, Fear not: for I will surely shew thee kindness for Jonathan thy father's sake, and will restore thee all the land of Saul thy father; and thou shalt eat bread at my table continually. 2 Samuel 9: 1-7

Here is a young man who had a beautiful life devastated. In one day his grandfather was killed. And on the same day his father died. Amidst his woes on the same day, his babysitter dropped him and the young man suffered physical disability. Three generations destroyed in one day.

Mephibosheth, lost his grandfather, his father, and became a cripple on the same day. In all of these troubling circumstances, life was not over for Mephibosheth. He kept on living until the day the king favored him and restored to him all his grandfather and father's riches. Though he was disable, the Lord favored him.

My dear brother and sisters, sometimes in life our situations and conditions may not change but God is able to give us the grace to keep going.

For this thing I besought the Lord thrice, that it might depart from me. And he said unto me, My grace is sufficient for thee: for my strength is made perfect in weakness. Most gladly therefore will I rather glory in my infirmities, that the power of Christ may rest upon me. Therefore I take pleasure in infirmities, in reproaches, in necessities, in persecutions, in distresses for Christ's sake: for when I am weak, then am I strong. 2 Corinthians 12: 8-10

Let's pray. Please say this prayer with me aloud. Lord Jesus I pray according to Your word, that by Your stripes I am healed. Please give me the faith, and the grace to keep trusting you until I receive my healing. Lord, I pray that just like those in the Bible who did not receive their healing but you gave them the grace to hold on and to keep living. I pray that you give me that same grace to keep on living, regardless. In Jesus name's, Amen.

CHAPTER 5

LOSS OF JOB, BUSINESS OR CAREER

Today, we live in a time and season where anything can happen, good or bad. It is my prayer that everything works out together for your good.
And we know that all things work together for good to them that love God, to them who are the called according to his purpose. Romans 8:28

This chapter deals with the danger of losing a job, a business, or a career. A loss of job for anyone working can pose a serious challenge especially for those who are breadwinners or those whose only source of livelihood and survival is through their job. Please understand that I believe that God is our source, however, I am dealing with the truth and the

reality of the loss of job. Not disrespecting any geographical location, a loss of job, business and or career is a serious business anywhere in the world you live. It can pose a devastating effect on individuals and family life.

> God is our source for living; our jobs, business and career is a means

I am especially concerned about those who live in the underdeveloped countries, where there is nothing called unemployment benefits when you loose a job. No bankruptcy shelter when a business fails or other viable options when the career we went to school for and have worked for a long time is no more. These can be very challenging and difficult times for anyone.

Losing a job, business or career in a developed country can be very devastating. It transcends into another story and drama all on its own. Since many of us in first world countries are a few paychecks away from losing our homes, our cars from repossession, and sometimes being pushed to the brink of collecting government assistance and at worse receive handouts just to make ends meet. Because of the credit system in developed countries, many of us buy things and live on credit. Our homes, cars, furniture, and other electronic and technology gadgets are acquired through credits. Therefore, when one loses a job or the business closes or the career is no longer thriving, our monthly expenditure is so overwhelming that we cannot survive; ultimately we begin to lose our things because we cannot continue to make the required payments.

I am neither a financial expert, nor am I trying to give you financial counsel in this narrative. All I am doing here is to address the real challenges and difficulties associated with losing a job, business or career. However, I will like to say this we need to cut our coats according to our sizes and learn to live within our means so that during difficult times, we can easily manage or be helped. Because some of you live with extravagance and largess, when you lose a job, it is not easy for you to manage things or be helped.

> Cut your coat according to your size.

For which of you, intending to build a tower, sitteth not down first, and counteth the cost, whether he have sufficient to finish it? Lest haply, after he hath laid the foundation, and is not able to finish it, all that behold it begin to mock him, Saying, This man began to build, and was not able to finish. Or what king, going to make war against another king, sitteth not down first, and consulteth whether he be able with ten thousand to meet him that cometh against him with twenty thousand? Luke 14: 28-31 *Wisdom is the principal thing; therefore get wisdom: and with all thy getting get understanding.* Proverbs 4:7

As mentioned earlier, sometimes I wonder whether it is easier for those who live in the underdeveloped world, since they live on cash and carry. And when they loose a job what they have acquired is somewhat safe. It is their survival and progress that is seriously threatened. I guess every situation comes with its own advantages and disadvantages…Just my thought.

I encourage you today and prepare your mind to understand that people do loose their jobs, businesses do fail and careers can be terminated. And when that happens, the attendant problems and other challenges that comes alongside losing your means of income can be minimized if you don't lose hope and have the courage to get back up after you have been bruised and knocked down. Many people's lives and stories have changed for the worse after their businesses have failed or have lost their job or career.

I have been anointed and graced by God to write and encourage you to get back up and begin again. If you are still living after the loss of a job, the collapse of a successful business, and the termination of a lucrative career, I write to encourage and exalt you that you can begin again.

A living dog is better than a dead lion.

I can only imagine how someone feels or be affected after working very hard on a job for many years and finally you are fired.. Investing all you have in a business and still couldn't work or losing a career you have built over many precious years is truly a life disaster. Each of these scenarios is

> The past is the PAST, the present is NOW, live it! The future is yet, PREPARE FOR IT.

possible and can be devastating. But if you are still alive, you can begin again.

Remember ye not the former things, neither consider the things of old. Behold, I will do a new thing; now it shall spring forth; shall ye not know it? I will even make a way in the wilderness, and rivers in the desert. Isaiah 43: 18-19

Let us pray. Please pray aloud with me. Lord Jesus. Please give me the peace to accept what has happened and give me the courage and strength to arise and begin again. I pray for your blessings and favor to find another good job, please open doors for another prosperous business opportunity and give me a better career in Jesus' name, Amen.

CHAPTER 6

SCHOOL DROPOUTS AND FAILURES

Not as though I had already attained, either were already perfect: but I follow after, if that I may apprehend that for which also I am apprehended of Christ Jesus. Brethren, I count not myself to have apprehended: but this one thing I do, forgetting those things which are behind, and reaching forth unto those things which are before, I press toward the mark for the prize of the high calling of God in Christ Jesus. Philippians 3:12-14

Dropping out of school or failing a major exam can affect someone's life. It can even hinder or discourage you from going back to school or applying to retake that exam.

> It doesn't matter how many times your fail, one pass can erase every failure.

Some of you reading this book may have dropped out of school and have lost the courage and strength to go back again. Some of you may have failed an exam or major test, maybe not even once or twice, and you have lost all hope to retest, or begin studying again for the exam. I will like to use my pastoral grace, I have prayed over this chapter like every other chapter with some seriousness and it is my belief that you are not reading this book and this chapter now by accident. If you will finish reading this chapter, believe in your heart that all things are possible to them that believe and pray with me in faith. I boldly declare you will pass that exam this time around in Jesus' name.

> It is not a shame to try and fail and keep on trying until you pass. It is a shame to give

And Elijah said unto Ahab, Get thee up, eat and drink; for there is a sound of abundance of rain. So Ahab went up to eat and to drink. And Elijah went up to the top of Carmel; and he cast himself down upon the earth, and put his face between his knees, And said to his servant, Go up now, look toward the sea. And he went up, and looked, and said, There is nothing. And he said, Go again seven times. And it came to pass at the seventh time, that he said,

Behold, there ariseth a little cloud out of the sea, like a man's hand. And he said, Go up, say unto Ahab, Prepare thy chariot, and get thee down that the rain stop thee not. And it came to pass in the meanwhile, that the heaven was black with clouds and wind, and there was a great rain. And Ahab rode, and went to Jezreel. And the hand of the Lord was on Elijah; and he girded up his loins, and ran before Ahab to the entrance of Jezreel. 1 Kings 18: 41-46

> No one is permitted to give up, everyone is encouraged to hold on.

In the scripture above, the prophet Elijah had to pray several times and at first it looks like he failed the first time and the second time but he kept

praying and he received his breakthrough. We too can do the same, keep pressing until you make it.

And he cometh to Bethsaida; and they bring a blind man unto him, and besought him to touch him. And he took the blind man by the hand, and led him out of the town; and when he had spit on his eyes, and put his hands upon him, he asked him if he saw ought. And he looked up, and said, I see men as trees, walking. After that he put his hands again upon his eyes, and made him look up: and he was restored, and saw every man clearly. And he sent him away to his house, saying, neither go into the town, nor tell it to any in the town. Mark 8: 22-26

In the gospel according to Mark, Jesus taught us a profound lesson in scriptures. Even Jesus had to touch the blind man twice for his vision to be restored. The first time may seem like a failure, Jesus had touched the blind man's eyes and asked him if he could see and the bling man responded by saying he was not seeing properly and Jesus had to touch his eyes again. You too can begin again.
As I conclude this chapter, let's deal with each of these subjects one at a time.

Many find themselves in the drop out category of life. Drop out of high school, college or university, or a program. The level or program you drop out from does not really matter because you can always begin again.

You may drop out, but don't give out.

Many potential and promising future are held hostage at the dropout stage. Until you stand up and step back into the game, you will not become what you were created to be.

Please permit me to share my story with you. I dropped out of North Lake Community College in Irving, TX in 2004. In 2006, I found the courage to begin again by enrolling at a Christian University to pursue my education in Christian Ministry. In 2008, I graduated with a bachelor's degree in Theology. I continued studying and in 2010, I graduated with a master's degree in Christian Counseling. This initial drop out pressed on and today I am proud to share that by the blessings of the Lord, in 2013, I earned a doctorate degree in Christian Counseling.

My dear friends all I'm trying to say is this, I dropped out but I did not stay out. I got up and began again. This book is heavily anointed and loaded with truths and real life experiences to help encourage you to begin again. I know that there are no two persons or situations are the same, but one thing I know is that we serve the same God. He is not a respecter of persons. What He does for one, He can do for another. Come on, get up and get back in school. I am praying for you. You can begin again.

Failing a major exam or test. There are many people than you can imagine who get stuck in this stage of life because they fail a major exam or test.

> Failure is not final.

Through must of our educational journey, many of us may have failed a quiz, a test, exam or even a course. But what I'm trying to address here is more than that. I am talking about major exams that people need to move to the next level such as entrance exam to enter a particular field or program.

Let's take the nursing field for a better example. You take all your prerequisites and pass and enter the registered nursing program. And you go to school for two hard and challenging years. At the end you completing the course, take the school final exams and pass. You registered for the state board exams for your license. You take that final exam and fail, not once, not twice, maybe several times. And discouragement and broken dreams set in, and you just walk away and give up. Life at this point can be very devastating to say the least. All the money, the studies and sacrifices and pain flashes in your face. And you begin to say maybe it was not meant to be, and you give up.

I write to challenge and encourage you that you can begin again and pass that exam by the help of God in Jesus name. I have come across few people in my life who were in these situations and I encouraged them and prayed with them that they can begin again. I helped them re-register for their exams, study for the exam and with joy in my heart, I share with you dear readers, that they went on to pass those exams and many of them are enjoying the fruit of their labor because they dare to begin again.

Let's pray. Please say this prayer with me aloud. Lord Jesus. I pray you give me the strength to bounce back from this drop out. Help me to get up and begin again. I pray for wisdom and understanding to face my fear and the challenge of re-taking the exams again. Lord Jesus please help me to pass this time. In Jesus name's, Amen.

CHAPTER 7
RELOCATION

The steps of a good man are ordered by the Lord: and he delighteth in his way. Psalms 37:23

Relocation is a tricky aspect of life because it can be a blessing or a curse. When the Lord impressed upon my heart to write this book on new beginnings, I envisioned a book with five chapters. As I planned the book, God told me that since 8 is the prophetic number of new beginnings, I should write 8 chapters, symbolizing new beginnings. As I pray for revelation and knowledge, the subject of relocation came down to me.

When we look back in our lives or even about others we know, it is clear that relocation has blessed and changed many individuals and family lives for the better. Maybe some of you reading this book has benefitted and blessed from relocation. But the contrary can also be true tha there arc others or even you whose life was severely affected and changed for the worse because of that one decision you made to relocate..

I do not take relocation lightly in life. Regardless of your geographical location, God can bless you from wherever you find yourself. It is also very serious and true that you may miss out on your blessings and destiny because of location. Everyone planning on locating or relocating must seriously pray for divine directions. May the Lord order you step in Jesus' name.

Order my steps in thy word: and let not any iniquity have dominion over me. Deliver me from the oppression of man: so will I keep thy precepts. Make thy face to shine upon thy servant; and teach me thy statutes. Rivers of waters run down mine eyes, because they keep not thy law. Psalms 119: 133-136

Now the Lord had said unto Abram, Get thee out of thy country, and from thy kindred, and from thy father's house, unto a land that I will shew thee:

And I will make of thee a great nation, and I will bless thee, and make thy name great; and thou shalt be a blessing: And I will bless them that bless thee, and curse him that curseth thee: and in thee shall all families of the earth be blessed. So Abram departed, as the Lord had spoken unto him; and Lot went with him: and Abram was seventy and five years old when he departed out of Haran. And Abram took Sarah his wife, and Lot his brother's son, and all their substance that they had gathered, and the souls that they had gotten in Haran; and they went forth to go into the land of Canaan; and into the land of Canaan they came. And Abram passed through the land unto the place of Sichem, unto the plain of Moreh. And the Canaanite was then in the land. And the Lord appeared unto Abram, and said, Unto thy seed will I give this land: and there builded he an altar unto the Lord, who appeared unto him. Genesis 12:1-7

Without trying to sound preachy, let me bring to your attention a few very important points from the text. As a careful Bible student, you will see that Abram's destiny in God was tied to his relocation *"get thee out of your country, from your*

> Stop following people who God has not asked you to follow.

family and from your father's house to a land that I will show you." Point number 2, Lot was not supposed to be a part of that relocation, so you can already see Lot giving or having problems.

Abram became our father of faith because of his

> Be in the right place at the right time.

obedience to God to relocate.

I pray for you too that as you stay where God wants you to be, He will locate you and bless you because of obedience.

And Elijah the Tishbite, who was of the inhabitants of Gilead, said unto Ahab, As the Lord God of Israel liveth, before whom I stand, there shall not be dew nor rain these years, but according to my word. And the word of the Lord came unto him, saying, get thee hence, and turn thee eastward, and hide thyself by the brook Cherith that is before Jordan. And it shall be, that thou shalt drink of the brook; and I have commanded the ravens to feed thee there. So he went and did according unto the word of the Lord: for he went and dwelt by the brook Cherith, that is before Jordan. And the ravens brought him bread and flesh in the morning, and bread and flesh in the evening; and he drank of the brook. And it came to pass after a while, that the brook dried up, because there had been no rain in the land. 1 Kings 17: 1-7

From the verses above you would find this revelation that God told Elijah to relocate to a place, a location where "He, God" will bless, protect and provide for him. He obeyed, relocated and God blessed, protected and provided for him. I pray that you are coming along with me. When

God's plans for that location were expired, He told Elijah to relocate.

And the word of the Lord came unto him, saying, Arise, get thee to Zarephath, which belongeth to Zidon, and dwell there: behold, I have commanded a widow woman there to sustain thee. So he arose

> Don't stay in a place when God instructs you to leave.

and went to Zarephath. And when he came to the gate of the city, behold, the widow woman was there gathering of sticks: and he called to her, and said, Fetch me, I pray thee, a little water in a vessel, that I may drink. And as she was going to fetch it, he called to her, and said, Bring me, I pray thee, a morsel of bread in thine hand. And she said, As the Lord thy God liveth, I have not a cake, but an handful of meal in a barrel, and a little oil in a cruse: and, behold, I am gathering two sticks, that I may go in and dress it for me and my son, that we may eat it, and die. And Elijah said unto her, Fear not; go and do as thou hast said: but make me thereof a little cake first, and bring it unto me, and after make for thee and for thy son. For thus saith the Lord God of Israel, The barrel of meal shall not waste, neither shall the cruse of oil fail, until the day that the Lord sendeth rain upon the earth. And she went and did according to the saying of Elijah: and she, and he, and her house, did eat many days. And the barrel of meal wasted not, neither did the cruse of oil fail, according to the word of the Lord, which he spake by Elijah. 1 Kings 17: 8-16

If you are hanging out with me I believe you can clearly see from the scripture above how obeying God's instructions as it relates to locations and relocations can be a blessing if we obey His voice. Our location and or relocation can bless us but also be a blessing to our families and others. Elijah was not only blessed, but by his obedience to relocate, a widow, her son and her household was spared,

Relocation can make you or break you.

sustained and blessed during a severe time of famine.

Don't relocate because of pressure, people or influence, relocate because you have prayed about it and God is leading you.

When God relocates you, people will locate you.

Finally, let me leave you with this masterpiece account from the Bible concerning our Lord and Savior Jesus Christ and how location and relocation played out in His life.

And when they were departed, behold, the angel of the Lord appeareth to Joseph in a dream, saying, Arise, and take the young child and his mother, and flee into Egypt, and be thou there until I bring thee word: for Herod will seek the young child to destroy him. When he arose, he took the young child and his mother by night, and departed into Egypt: And was there until the death of Herod: that it might be fulfilled which was spoken of the Lord by the prophet, saying, Out of Egypt have I called my son. Matthew 2: 13-15

When you read a full account in Matthew 2:1,, you will notice that Herold was the King in Bethlehem, Judea, and a very wicked King who persecuted and killed a lot of Christians. The wise men came asking where is He who is born King of the Jews? For we have seen His star. When Herold heard this, he was troubled and plotted to kill Jesus. The text above shows how God directed Joseph to relocate with the Christ child Jesus for protection.

Location and relocation matters.

But when Herod was dead, behold, an angel of the Lord appeareth in a dream to Joseph in Egypt, Saying, Arise, and take the young child and his mother, and go into the land of Israel: for they are dead which sought the young child's life. And he arose, and took the young child and his mother, and came into the land of Israel. But when he heard that Archelaus did reign in Judaea in the room of his father Herod, he was afraid to go thither: notwithstanding, being warned of God in a dream, he turned aside into the parts of Galilee: And he came and dwelt in a city called Nazareth: that it might be fulfilled which was spoken by the prophets, He shall be called a Nazarene. Matthew 2: 19-23

In this account, Joseph was divinely directed in a dream by God to relocate Jesus to Israel because those who sought to kill Jesus were there (Herold). I pray you will not miss your location in life.

Now let's conclude with a true real life stories I was taught about two families who relocated. One moved from Africa to England, and the other from Africa to America. (Please understand that I know that Africa is not a country; it is a continent, but I'm trying not to be specific in this story.)

When Michael relocated from Africa, he did everything he could do to relocate his fiancé and two sons to the United Kingdom. Eventually they were granted a permission to relocate. Within a short period of time, the couples got married and had two more children. The family was successful. They were well established and succeeded in all they put their hands to do. Today, as I write their story, they are doing well and have helped many of their families and friends back home and even brought some over to England. Relocation for this family worked out well and was a blessing to many. It is my prayer that no matter what, your story will have a happy ending.

Unlike the first family, the second family, which relocated from Africa to America wasn't as successful. In this family the couple was already married and the wife came over on a program with three kids, living the husband behind. After three years of trying hard, the wife succeeded in bringing the husband over. So many things happened that I am not a liberty to share, due to the relocation. But let's say, it wasn't the best of relocations imagined from a third world country into a first world. Within barely three years, the couple separated and filed for a divorce. The fight was so bad that it could be aptly tagged as the "wars of wars" After their divorce an allegation was made against the father and husband by one of the three children and he was arrested and deported. His marriage, children and life were all destroyed due to relocation. Let us be careful as we relocate and pray not to be on the losing end of relocation.

I know someone reading this chapter would be tempted to think that relocating from a third world in pursuit of a greener pasture can never be wrong. I write to say don't be hasty in your expectations without the Lord leading you. All that glitters is not gold. There is a way that seems right onto a man, but the end is of destruction. Some relocation can destroy people, families, and the future. Pray about relocation.

I have seen people who have relocated voluntarily or involuntarily go through very difficult times. I am writing to strengthen and encourage you that if you are hurt or dislocated because of relocation you can begin again. Many have lost jobs, homes, lands, and families just to relocate and they are now going through tough times. I'm praying for you that my God would reverse the hard times and settle you wherever you are. Hold on, all is not lost there is hope once there is life. You can begin again.

Let's pray. Please pray this prayer aloud with me. Lord Jesus, please give me the wisdom and understanding to relocate. Order my step oh Lord and direct my path. Father, pray that You help me settle as I have relocated already, forgive me and establish me. Father I pray that from today forward

You would order my step, direct my path as I relocate. Thank you Father, in Jesus' name I pray. Amen.

CHAPTER 8

LIFE HAPPENS

For a just man falleth seven times, and riseth up again: but the wicked shall fall into mischief. Proverbs 24: 16

This chapter is a very special chapter to me. As I age in life, I have come to understand by wisdom and experience that life happens. Life is not a straight line; it is full of twists and turns, ups and down. Hold on tight it can be a rough ride, sometimes it's like a rollercoaster; it takes you up and brings you down, sometimes it goes fast and at other times it goes slow.

We are therefore encouraged to prepare and plan well for life. I inspire you to plan and to fast and to pray, however, regardless of whether you plan or not, life still happens. In this life, there are the good, the bad, and the ugly. And at every given point in time one of them will show up. I'm writing this chapter to educate, encourage, and empower you that when life happens you can begin again.

Betrayals, disappointments, and setbacks are part of life. We need to be strong and very courageous in order to travel down this road called life.

Have not I commanded thee? Be strong and of a good courage; be not afraid, neither be thou dismayed: for the Lord thy God is with thee whithersoever thou goest. Joshua 1:9

Many people get stuck in life because life happens. Some people have refused to get up and go on because difficult circumstances in life have happened. Friends be not deceived, life will and do happen.

> When we get knocked down, we get back up, it's called life.

Just because you are a nice person or helpful and loyal to people neither exonerate nor guarantee you that life will not happen and that people will not hurt you. It pays to be good, helpful, sincere, loyal, and trustworthy in all that you involve yourself in - All of those are good qualities of life. It will help you but not stop life from happening and continuing its course. Remember, good is always good.

I have come across many fine people both young and old, who are stuck in life because of setbacks and disappointments. My dear reader, let's get real, setbacks and disappointments are all ingredients of life.

My brethren, count it all joy when ye fall into divers temptations; Knowing this, that the trying of your faith worketh patience. But let patience have her perfect work, that ye may be perfect and entire, wanting nothing. If any of you lack wisdom, let him ask of God, that giveth to all men liberally, and upbraideth not; and it shall be given him. James 1: 2-5

If you are reading this book and you are bitter and angry at life and people, because you perceive some semblance of unfairness and unjust towards you and have disappointed you; you have the right book in your hands. Shake it off! Life goes on and things do happen. Don't get stuck! Keep moving on. I am speaking to every situation we are faced with in life. Get up, shake it off, get over it and live life. If a few of us could come together and sit around a table to explain how life has happened to us, some of us would confess or admit that our case is way better off than others. However, the truth is, everyone's situation is different and everyone's problem is a problem.

Amongst the many gifts that I know the Lord has blessed me with, one of them is the gift of exaltation. As I write this chapter, I am strongly standing on that gift. Be encouraged and receive strength not just to endure life but to enjoy life. You will notice that the central theme in this book and every chapter is courage, wisdom and strength to begin again.

> The only person you have control over is you.

In my own life I have faced some serious disappointments and setbacks, but through it all, I persevered to succeed in life. I could have given up. I had every reason to but unfortunately I was not permitted to fail. I dropped out of school. Even though it was a personal setback to me, I did not allow it to negatively dictate my life. Hastily, I regrouped, found the strength and the courage to come back and begin again.

I always tell this immigration story and will forever tell this story regardless of my circumstances because it is dear to me. My immigration story changed my whole life, my worldview, and faith in God. I wish I could be very specific on so many of the narrative and offer you a deeper insight, but obviously for many reasons I cannot. Initially, I had a difficult time with my immigration status in the United States. For a decade, I went through setbacks and disappointments after disappointments as it relates to my permanent resident status in the

United States. Every program and everything that I tried to fix and regularized my status failed. It went so bad that when I applied for the Temporary Protective Status (TPS) that the government was granting freely and easily to many Liberians, I was denied. Really! Are you kidding me? At first, I was devastated. I couldn't get over it easily. And as funny as I would like to be now, I was devastated because life happened and took it course. May I just take the liberty to throw a little light on some of the seriousness of living in America today with out your immigration papers. You can't go to school, Work or even Drive. You are always looking over your shoulder. Let me share this one personal story with you. I was working with this company and it looks like someone made a comment that led our cooperate office to ask our H.R. Office to check and request for our immigration papers. It was a time like non other. Folks quited, some were fired because of immigration paper. As for me, due some connections I was allowed to work for 120day because of some story I told them. Those days were some of the worst days of my life. Because of the story I told them, every visitor who came into our building, I thought they were immigration officers and I knew all the exits because I was ready to escape. Talk about disappointments and setbacks, I had my own fair share, and this is just one area of my life.

I am laughing now as I write this story, but wasn't so when I had my disappointment. I went through some tough and difficult times that could have broken me and took me out of shape.

Like the old proverbial saying, "all that ends well is well". May I submit to you that during those hard times in my life, I never lost hope or gave up? Yes I was disappointed and sad but my hope did not disappear. I made a personal commitment to keep on trying even if I had to die trying. Today, I can joyfully say the Lord has granted me my heart desire and settled me in the United States of America. It can happen for you in different ways and areas of your life, just keep on pressing. Don't give in, don't give up. It is not over until it is over. Get up! You can begin again.

As I conclude this final chapter of "You Can Begin Again", I would like to close with two of my most beloved bible stories and characters.

Now it came to pass in the days when the judges ruled, that there was a famine in the land. And a certain man of Bethlehemjudah went to sojourn in the country of Moab, he, and his wife, and his two sons. And the name of the man was Elimelech, and the name of his wife Naomi, and the name of his two sons Mahlon and Chilion, Ephrathites of Bethlehemjudah. And they came into the country of Moab, and continued there. And Elimelech Naomi's husband died; and she was left, and her two sons. And they took them wives of the women of Moab; the name of the one was Orpah, and the name of the other Ruth: and they dwelled there about ten years. And Mahlon and Chilion died also both of them; and the woman was left of her two sons and her husband. Ruth 1: 1-5

In the scripture above, you will find the story of this beautiful young lady called Ruth and how she got married to the love of her life and the future was bright and colorful and she could not ask for more but life happened. First, she lost her father in law, and then her brother in law and then finally her husband passed away. Talking about setbacks and disappointments, this was the mother of all setbacks.

So Boaz took Ruth, and she was his wife: and when he went in unto her, the Lord gave her conception, and she bare a son. And the women said unto Naomi, Blessed be the Lord, which hath not left thee this day without a kinsman, that his name may be famous in Israel. And he shall be unto thee a restorer of thy life, and a nourisher of thine old age: for thy daughter in law, which loveth thee, which is better to thee than seven sons, hath born him. And Naomi took the child, and laid it in her bosom, and became nurse unto it. And the women her neighbors gave it a name, saying, There is a son born to

Naomi; and they called his name Obed: he is the father of Jesse, the father of David. Ruth 4:13-17

We can learn from this text that Ruth found the courage; she received strength to begin again. According to this text, Ruth picked up her pieces and moved on. She got married not to any ordinary guy but to the richest guy in the east. And she gave birth to a child through whose lineage our Lord and Savior Jesus Christ was born. Please receive faith and encouragement to trust God that you can begin again.

Another compelling story that will encourage you to begin again is about a man called Job. He was a good and righteous man. The Bible says he was one of the wealthiest men in all of the east. Nevertheless, one day, life happened. You can read this account in Job Chapter 1 and 2. In a single day, Job lost all of his possessions and his children. Have you ever asked the question, why do bad things happen to good people? This is the ideal story that no matter how good and righteous we are, life happens to all men. So the story continues in Chapter 2 with Job losing his health and his wife tempting him to curse God and die. But Job refused because he believed that as long as he had life, there was hope. You can believe that and it is not over until it is over because you can always begin again. The story ends in Job Chapter 42: 10.

And the Lord turned the captivity of Job, when he prayed for his friends: also the Lord gave Job twice as much as he had before. Job 42:10

You will notice that Job received double for his trouble because he dared to believe and trust God. He was able to begin again and I speak and declare that you too can begin again.

Sometimes, you don't get to marry the love of your life. Sometimes in life the story is not always a happy ending and at other times, you don't get all the breaks we expect in life. You get sick. Your relationships grew apart. Once happily married couples divorce. Yes. What I am trying to say here is that bad things do happen to good people. Life happens but you can begin again. People get down in life with all kinds of garbage. As I move towards the conclusion of this book, I want to remind you that life is real, setbacks and disappointments are part of life. But don't give up, get up, and begin again.

Not as though I had already attained, either were already perfect: but I follow after, if that I may apprehend that for which also I am apprehended of Christ Jesus. Brethren, I count not myself to have apprehended: but this one thing I do, forgetting those things which are behind, and reaching forth unto those things which are before, I press toward the mark for the prize of the high calling of God in Christ Jesus. Philippians 3:12-14

These are few practical steps I would like to share with you in order to begin again.

1. Believe in God.
2. Believe that once there is life there is hope.
3. Encourage yourself.
4. Ask God for help.

5. Get up and begin again.

Let's pray. Please pray this prayer aloud with me. Lord Jesus. Please give me the wisdom, the knowledge, the grace and the courage to face life and to keep on keeping on. By wisdom and experience, I have read and learned from this book that life is not a straight line, help me oh God during the twist and turns in life, that I may hold on just like Job until my change come. Please give me the grace and the power and the understanding to begin again. In Jesus' name I pray. Amen.